ITIAHaiti

501(c)(3) NONPROFIT ORGANIZATION

Innovation of the Territory by Itiahists Active of Haiti

Artistic and Literary Organization

Philosophy, Articles of Organization - Project Idea

PREFACE

This book is for everyone who would like to know more about ITIAHaiti as a 501(c)(3) Nonprofit Organization, specifically for its members. Most of the time, organizations don't disclose their vision, mission, and objectives to the public so that people don't steal their project ideas, nor copy their statutes.

At ITIAHaiti, we do things differently, we believe in a society where everyone has to know the path to become self-reliant. This book will guide you to discover the best Haitian youth nonprofit organizations in the world, and we invite you to be part of the board of "Innovation of the

Territory by Itiahists Active of Haiti (ITIAHaiti) as well.

Time plays against us, and we cannot reach our goal without you. Please, stand together to promote our youth, inclusion, and social cohesion. By perusing our philosophy, articles of organization, and our project idea, you already plant a tree for the development of Haiti. Feel free to join us as adherents or honorary members.

Wilson Thelimo Louis,

President/CEO of ITIAHaiti

Welcome aboard!

PHILOSOPHY OF ITIAHAITI

At a time when Haitian literature is almost dead, contemporary poets think it is their duty to revive Haitian letters. In search for national literary identity, these writers gathered under a literary organization called ITIAHaiti or Innovation of the Territory by Itiahists Active of Haiti. Considered the first Haitian literary doctrine of the 21st century, itiahism was born out of a group of committed young writers who were willing to sacrifice themselves by raising their hands to say no to any form of injustice that occurred during their existence. This revulsion to injustice was channeled into a literary movement which emerged on July 12, 2008, with young poets forming a literary club to encourage poetry and perform plays in the Haitian southern city of Les Cayes. The idea later expanded on social media to give birth to a literary school exalting the Haitian heritage. The primary purpose of ITIAHaiti was to promote the clarity of literature that highlights translates and reflects all realities of Haiti. It promotes a licit, teachable and original literature while advocating innovative poetry.

Itiahism believes in the promotion of stylish prose and supports other associations that are working for the development of Haitian culture. His theorists aim to make the territory their inspirational source. Itiahists use their pen to paint their country's beauty and to focus on various facets of their society. According to them, social nuances and cohesion are the ingredients which will make Haiti truly beautiful and project the depth of its history. Itiahism gleans ideas from the moral atmosphere in order to synchronize the natives with their homeland. Their philosophy of self-reliance elevates the human being as the god of his heaven and the honey of his bee to empower the true meaning of existence. Its doctrine of making men and women the materials of their masterpiece binds all literary and philosophical doctrines of the centuries which are questioned the ecstasy of surreal. The history of itiahism is completely inseparable from Haiti whence it comes. It synchronizes with the first independent Negro Republic in the world, the condition of an actual pirated sovereignty and the future of a powerful country. Itiahism teaches pragmatism and self-reliance as the best avenues to Haiti's success.

Itiahism would surely be acceptable if it had, as an immediate consequence the action of eliminating from history the intruders of the philosophies of all doctrines, their manners, and customs which make, on one hand, the basis of the Haitian belief and on the other hand, the power to globalize Haitian creole as revolutionary language. Itiahists cannot be influenced by any other culture; they fight to promote their works everywhere in the world. Their externalizations are exerted on each faculty like spirit on flesh and are oriented towards the right way so that they do not astray.

Writers of this doctrine do not quarrel, these patriots are synthetic, focus and aesthetic. They speak less and say more. This doctrine tends to defend typical Haitian literature that is focused on universality. It is a form of militancy that is considered a weapon against the devastating powers that plunge the country into intellectual chaos, where Haiti's sons and daughters are forced to go into exile in search of subsistence. This drives the youth, the powerful force, the energy and the seed of this ancestral land to lose interest in its own culture. Itiahists are fighters to the extreme for freedom and the scrupulous respect of the human being. The ideal of itiahism can be summed up thus: the promotion of the Haitian people through radical change and meaningful progress.

For the Itiahists, defending their cultural identity is one of the winning strategies, in addition to educating and engaging the elite to save their homeland. Describing the misery of a zombie people of their period through their works and exalting the beauty of what remains good is a psychological asset used to motivate this great nation and to take up his torch at last; thus, these enthusiasts are alarmed to awaken poetry, restore the landscapes, sing their country and make their pens a therapy for the traumatized and an assault against the corrupt leader. Itiahism is neither a poem, nor a play, nor a novel either. Being creative, the Itiahists adopt their own style and are free in their works. The Itiahists do not destroy, they build. They do not just blame, they advise. They do not distort but transform. They do not only protest but propose new ideas. Itiahists undresses while caressing, harmonizing and perfecting in everything. Itiahism lays a (hyphen) bridge between a neglected past and an alarming present to build the future of Haitian society.

Wilson Thelimo Louis,

President/CEO of ITIAHaiti

Articles of

Organization

CHAPTER I

IDENTIFICATION OF ITIAHaiti

ART. 1 - THE NAME – VISION AND MISSION

With a vision of an autonomous Haiti, ITIAHaiti, or Innovation of the Territory by Itiahists Active of Haiti is founded in July 12th, 2008 in the southern city of Les Cayes, in Haiti. It is a Nonprofit Organization whose mission is to revive the Haitian culture while coaching youth to build their leadership through arts.

Art. 2 - REGISTERED OFFICE

ITIAHaiti is registered in August 22nd in the United States of America and is headquartered at 45 Stanbro Street, Hyde Park, MA 02136. It can be moved to any other city in the country at the express request of the General Assembly.

Art. 3 - JURISDICTION

The jurisdiction of Innovation of the Territory by Itiahists Active of Haiti (ITIAHaiti) extends throughout the United States of America.

Art. 4 - OBJECTIVES OF ITIAHaiti

— Empower youth to become self-reliant and work to strengthen their intrinsic capacities

— Encourage the flowering of a culture that paints, translates and reflects the realities of Haiti

— Provide moral and ethical assistance to its members

— Promote a healthy, teachable and original literature while advocating for innovative poetry that revives Haitian myths

— Promote Haitian Creole, youth, inclusion, and social cohesion through arts

— Restore confidence in youth through behavior change training seminars and leadership

— Support associations working to develop Haitian culture

— Teach conflict management and the concept of fair play through arts to different communities.

Art. 5 - MEANS

ITIAHaiti proposes to meet its goals by the following means:

— Promote the participation and integration of its members in international funding organizations and non-governmental organizations interested in its statutes

— Subscribe to any action that strengthens each member's capacities and associations working with ITIAHaiti

Art. 6 - AFFILIATION OR REGROUP

ITIAHaiti is a non-governmental, non-denominational and apolitical non-profit organization working with other organizations, social groups and foundations sharing the same objectives and philosophies and evolving in the same spheres of activity, both national and international while safeguarding its independence.

CHAPTER II

MEMBERS OF ITIAHaiti

Art. 7 - CONDITIONS

To be a member of ITIAHaiti, you must:

— Respect and apply its statutes

— Sign internal regulations

— Understand its underlying philosophy and adopt it

Art. 8- CATEGORIES OF MEMBERS

There are three categories of members within ITIAHaiti:

a) Founding members

b) Adherent members

c) Honorary members.

Art. 9- FOUNDING MEMBERS

The founding members are those who took part in the various steps leading to the first constituent General Assembly of ITIAHaiti, voted on the statutes and signed the constitutive act. They may also be called active members, i.e. those who have regularly attended ITIAHaiti's meetings and activities and participated in official decision-making processes.

Art. 10- ADHERENT MEMBERS

Adherent members are those who have joined ITIAHaiti after submitting an application to the Board of Directors, either individually or as an association. They are also those who, for specific reasons, regularly take part only in the activities of ITIAHaiti and who contribute in one way or another to achieve the mission of ITIAHaiti.

Art. 11- HONORARY MEMBERS

Honorary members are the benefactors of ITIAHaiti or people who, in one way or another, have contributed financially and materially to execute projects or who are engaged in the pursuit of its objectives.

Art. 12 - ELECTION OF HONORARY MEMBERS

Upon the presentation of two members of the Board of Directors and after approval of the other members of the Board, any moral or physical person may be appointed Honorary Member of ITIAHaiti. The Honorary Member is exempt from payment of their subscription but does not have the right to vote in the General Assembly.

CHAPTER III

THE GENERAL ASSEMBLY

Art. 13- COMPOSITION

The General Assembly is made up of all members regularly registered and in good standing with ITIAHaiti.

Art. 14- ATTRIBUTIONS OF THE
GENERAL ASSEMBLY

ITIAHaiti is run by a Board of Directors under the control of the general assembly which is the supreme authority of the Artistic and Literary Organization. It meets once a year under the convocation of the President of ITIAHaiti. However, in case of an emergency and at the request of two-thirds of the council, a special convocation can be planned under extenuating circumstances. The attributions of the General Assembly are:

a) Oversee administration of ITIAHaiti affairs and its inner workings

b) Organize elections of members of the Board of Directors

c) Approve the organization's work plans, projects, and strategies

d) To make all necessary acts and take all dispositions that it considers opportune to the benefit of ITIAHaiti and which are not in opposition with the laws of the United States of America

e) Amend the present statutes.

Art. 15- QUORUM OF THE GENERAL ASSEMBLY

The quorum for the general meeting is two-thirds. If this quorum is not reached, the general meeting is postponed for one week. At this time, the general assembly is organized regardless of the number of people present.

CHAPTER IV

BOARD OF DIRECTORS

Art. 16- DIRECTION

The Board of Directors is composed of nine members and the relations between the different members of this Board are defined in the internal regulations.

Art. 17- COMPOSITION

The Board of Directors is composed of seven members:

1. President
2. Vice President
3. Secretary/Clerk
4. Assistant Secretary/Assistant Clerk
5. Treasurer/Chief Financial Officer (CFO)
6. Assistant CFO/Assistant Treasurer
7. Delegate
8. Advisor
9. Second Advisor

Art. 18- QUORUM OF THE BOARD OF DIRECTORS

The quorum of the Board of Directors is 50% +1 of all members. In case of an equality of votes, the vote of the President counts for two votes.

Art. 19- MEETINGS

The Board of Directors meets twice a month at its registered office or at any other place designated by members of the Board at the invitation of the President. Decisions are made either by vote or by consensus while seeking to develop collective leadership to facilitate harmony and understanding among Council members.

CHAPTER V

RESPONSIBILITIES OF THE BOARD OF DIRECTORS

ART. 20- RESPONSIBILITIES OF THE
BOARD OF DIRECTORS ARE:

a) Admit or suspend members of ITIAHaiti pending the final decision of the General Assembly

b) Determine the dates of general meetings

c) Institute any commissions and subcommittees necessary to study, discuss, promote or achieve objectives of ITIAHaiti

d) Receive and study all communications made to the Board of Directors and submit its report to the general meeting

e) Comply with decisions made during ordinary and extraordinary shareholders meetings

f) Submit to the General Assembly all questions that require a vote from the members, such as elections of members of the Board of Directors, request for alliance and change of strategies

g) Ensure application of regulations decreed by the General Assembly

h) Manage ITIAHaiti's bank accounts.

Art. 21- VOTING

Decisions made at Board of Directors meetings are taken by the majority of votes of present members. In case of equality, the President's vote counts for two votes. Election of members of the Board of Directors is done by secret ballot.

CHAPTER VI

TASKS OF MEMBERS OF THE BOARD

OF DIRECTORS

Art. 22- PRESIDENT

The President of ITIAHaiti's duties are as follows:

a) Convene the Board of Directors and ordinary and extraordinary general meetings

b) Coordinate and chair Board and general meetings

c) Notify interested parties of decisions taken in general assembly and supervise the operation of ITIAHaiti's activities

d) Prepare an agenda and submit it in advance to the board members

e) Be represented by the vice president in case of absence or impediment

f) Sign reports and important documents.

Art. 23- VICE PRESIDENT

The Vice President automatically replaces the President in case of impediment or absence. He/she also performs all prerogatives within his function and coordinates at the request of the President at appropriate times.

Art. 24- SECRETARY/CLERK

The Secretary/Clerk is responsible for activities and all correspondence of ITIAHaiti. He/she writes meeting reports of the general assembly and signs them for authentication. He/she is the guardian of all archives of the Artistic and Literary Organization and is in charge of training, education of ITIAHaiti members and associations with privileged relations with ITIAHaiti. Annually, she/he prepares work plans for board members training for approval.

Art. 25- ASSISTANT SECRETARY/ ASSISTANT CLERK

The Assistant Secretary/Assistant Clerk automatically replaces the secretary if he/she is unable to attend. She/he also performs all tasks associated with his/her function and acts on request of the Secretary at appointed times.

ART. 26- THE CHIEF FINANCIAL OFFICER/ TREASURER

He/she administers the property of ITIAHaiti and is also in charge of funds and as such must keep an exact account of financial transactions. She/he executes expenses under the supervision of the Board of Directors, usually signs the checks together with the President, reports on his/her administration to the general meeting by publishing an annual report of financial results, and prepares ITIAHaiti's operating and investment budget. However, it may happen that the financial operations of the Artistic and Literary Organization are so complex that it would be necessary to entrust the responsibility to a specialized service under its control.

ART. 27 ASSISTANT CHIEF FINANCIAL OFFICER/ASSISTANT TREASURER

The Assistant Chief Financial Officer/Assistant Treasurer automatically replaces the Chief Financial Officer/Treasurer if he/she is unable to manage a task. She/he also performs all tasks associated with his/her function and acts on request of the CFO at appointed times.

Art. 28- THE DELEGATE

He/she is responsible for the promotion and advertising of ITIAHaiti and to sell the image and policies of the Artistic and Literary Organization in matters of development. He/she is also the spokesperson for ITIAHaiti.

Art. 29- ADVISOR

The Advisor participates actively in all meetings as a member of the council and gives his/her opinion during decisions. The Advisor may be mandated by the council to represent the Artistic and Literary Organization where appropriate.

ART. 30- SECOND ADVISOR

The Second Advisor participates actively in all meetings as a member of the council and gives his/her opinion during decisions. The Second Advisor may be mandated by the council to represent the Artistic and Literary Organization where appropriate also.

Art. 31- REMUNERATION

The members of the Board of Directors are not entitled to any remuneration, except for travel expenses as well as those incurred by special assignments.

Art. 32- ELIGIBILITY

Any member who is in good standing with ITIAHaiti is eligible to be elected to the Board. Board members are eligible for re-election. An absent member may stand as a candidate if and only if he/she is represented at the nominating meeting by a duly authorized member on his/her behalf, under a procedure established by the election committee appointed by the Board of Directors.

Art. 33- DURATION OF THE MANDATE

Board of Directors members is elected to a four-year term. At the end of this term, all Board members are required to resign and submit their reports at the General Meeting. This formality does not prevent them from seeking a new mandate for the same position or for a different position.

CHAPTER VII

THE EXECUTIVE DIRECTORATE AND

ITS DUTIES

Art. 34-

The Executive Directorate is the technical-administrative body responsible for implementing the general policy of the Artistic and Literary Organization defined by the Board of Directors. As such, it ensures the continuity of the council.

Art. 35-

The Executive Directorate is under control of a qualified and experienced professional selected by the Board and given the title of Executive Director.

Art. 36-

The Executive Director works under the authority of the Board of Directors.

Art. 37-

The Vice Executive Director works under the authority of the Vice Directors.

Art. 38-

The executive director involves in the day-to-day operations of the organization. He/she hires, supervises, and motivates the staff of the nonprofit. The executive director works with the staff to develop policies to guide the organization and programs to fulfill its charitable purpose. She/he also keeps the board informed of what the organization is doing. The executive director attends board meetings and maintains open lines of communication with the Board of Directors.

Art. 39- GROUPS, COMMISSIONS

Groups and commissions are socio-administrative bodies responsible for the implementation of socio-cultural projects and the establishment of necessary service structures as defined in the objectives of ITIAHaiti to ensure monitoring, maintenance, and permanence of activities of the Artistic and Literary Organization in all its geographical territories. These entities work under the supervision of the Executive Director as defined by the Board Policy.

CHAPTER VIII

ELECTION METHODS AND CANDIDACY CONDITIONS

Art. 40-

Elections are held by direct suffrage every four years to elect members of the Board of Directors.

Art. 41-

To participate in elections, you must:

a) Have the will to help others

b) Be an active member for at least one year

c) Understand the philosophy of ITIAHaiti

Art.42-

The Executive Directorate forms an electoral commission responsible for organizing the elections. It may be composed of five members including three members representing the General Assembly.

Art. 43-

Once the electoral commission is formed, it adopts the electoral rules and procedures and ensures scrupulous compliance with said rules and established timetable.

Art. 41-

Candidates are elected by secret ballot by an absolute majority of votes of active members meeting in general assembly. Members can be re-elected if the vote is favorable.

Art. 44-

After having prepared the minutes of the General Assembly, the elected officials take office immediately after their election.

CHAPTER IX

ITIAHaiti's RESOURCES

Art.45-

ITIAHaiti's resources fall into two categories: ordinary and extraordinary.

a) Ordinary resources: contributions, subscription fees, local financing of projects and all socio-cultural activities. The annual fees for each member amount to $15.00

b) Extraordinary resources: donations to the Artistic and Literary Organization by certain members and public or private organizations, both national and international.

CHAPTER X

SUSPENSION, EXPULSION, AND

REINTEGRATION

Art. 46- RESIGNATION

A member or group of an affiliated association may, within the time prescribed for that purpose, submit his/her resignation to the Board of Directors. This resignation becomes effective when it is notified in writing to the President of the Board. A resigning member immediately loses all rights and privileges from the date of resignation.

Art.47- SUSPENSION OF A MEMBER

The Board of ITIAHaiti may suspend any member who:

a) Refuses to comply with commitments made to the Artistic and Literary Organization

b) Inflicts serious damage on ITIAHaiti

c) Neglects or refuses to comply with decisions of the general meeting or of the Board within the scope of its attributions

d) Does not respect the philosophy of itiahism.

Art.48 - APPEAL FOR SUSPENSION

a) A suspended member of the Artistic and Literary Organization may appeal by applying the following procedures:

b) Within thirty clear days after the decision, the suspended member may appeal in writing to an arbitrator chosen by mutual agreement with the President of the Board. After this period, the member is considered to be expelled from ITIAHaiti.

c) The arbitrator thus appointed determines the procedure and hears the parties before deciding the dispute. His/her decision must be rendered as soon as possible. If the arbitrator maintains the suspension, the suspended member may appeal a second time to the general meeting. The dispute will be heard in extraordinary General Assembly to deliberate upon definitively. This procedure lasts 60 days.

Art. 49- REINTEGRATION OF A MEMBER

Only a resigning member can be reinstated into ITIAHaiti. To be reinstated, the resigning member must make a request in writing to the President of the Board of Directors.

CHAPTER XI

GENERAL PROVISIONS

Art. 50 PROCEDURES

The procedural operations code of ITIAHaiti applies to the holding of general meetings and to define the attributes of the Board of Directors. In the case of unforeseen situations or difficulties of interpretation, the General Assembly will determine the procedure to follow.

CHAPTER XII

AMENDMENT, DISSOLUTION, AND

LIQUIDATION

Art. 51- AMENDMENT OF STATUTES

Any proposal having the effect of suspending or modifying the present statutes, in whole or in part, must be presented by the General Assembly of members by notice of motion. This notice of motion cannot be considered until it has been read at an extraordinary general meeting and supported by at least five members of the Board of Directors. Any changes to the statutes of this Artistic and Literary Organization will only come into effect after having been approved by a simple majority of members of the General Assembly.

Art. 52- DISSOLUTION OF ITIAHaiti

The voluntary dissolution of ITIAHaiti cannot be envisaged as long as there are members willing to occupy all the positions of the Board of Directors.

Art. 53- LIQUIDATION

In the event of dissolution, the remaining property will be distributed to similar Artistic and Literary Organizations.

FOUNDING MEMBERS OF ITIAHAITI

In Boston, Massachusetts, on August 12, 2019, in the 243rd year since the independence of the United States of America; following are the signatures of the founding members:

Aldajuste Mistral – Auguste Romelus – Berline Ramcesse Charlotin– Billy Pierre – Claudy Fanord - Cherlin Simon – Claude Sévère – Dieula Beaucamp – Emmanuel Marion – Emmanuel Romelus – Emmeline Menard - Franky Célestin – Fritz Gerard Davidson Dieu – Emmanuel Georges Mathieu – Esther Louis Lalanne - Guillaume Decopain – Hugens Lygens - Jacques Alciné – James Francisque – James

Micaël Pierre – Jean-Bertrand Oriza - Jean Bradley Derenoncourt - Jean Brenus Brezeau – Jean Jonel Alexandre – Jean Markens Clervil – Jean Philippe Desmornes – Jean Simon Léger – Jean Smith Auguste – Jean-Jacques Plaisimond – Jeanne Yveline Neptune – Jessica Nazaire – Jessey Rene Louis – John Youky Laguerre - Junior Malbranche – Kenzy François – Louigens Istrop – Lyvita Cazeau – Makenzy Felix – Marconi Arthur Dèsrouillères – Marie Cécile Gilet – Marie Joane Dimanche – Maryns Starline Labossière – Max Getro Chavannes – Mendiny Joseph – Métélus Forde – Metichella Altema – Michel Denis - Michena Elysée – Onel Berrette – Osny Altema - Pedro Walter Bellabre – Pierre André Joachim – Pierre Frantz Maxi – Pierre Jodelin Léger – Pierre Roberson-Roland

Neptune – Robentz Dorvil – Rodney Kelly Cornet – Rose Carmelle Fortuné – Rosemine Jean - Jacques – Rousselor René – Tisselin Noezil – Venel Senat – Watson Messeroux – Webert Joujoute – Wilguens Altema – Wilson Thelimo Louis - Winchel Chérismé - Windy Coudo – Wolson Louis – Yves Mary Jean.

CONSTITUTIVE ACT

August 12th, 2019, in the 243rd year since independence of the United States of America at noon; we, the founding members of this Artistic and Literary Organization, located at 45, Stanbro Street, Boston, MA, 02136, USA, have taken upon ourselves to create a non-profit organization called "Innovation of the Territory by Itiahists Active of Haiti," adopting the acronym: ITIAHaiti.

To this end, after having signed the constituent documents of the Artistic and Literary Organization, the members present at this general assembly elected a Board of Directors of eleven members with a mandate of four years in order to work on the implementation strategies that can lead to the achievement of the objectives set out in the Articles of Organization in the United States of America.

Finally, the questions of general interest have principally focused on the commitment of these advocates for the advancement of the said Artistic and Literary Organization called "ITIAHaiti or Innovation of the Territory by the Active Itiahists of Haiti." The Board of Directors is composed of the following members:

Wilson Thelimo Louis, President/CEO

Yves Mary Jean, Vice President

Emmeline A. Menard, Clerk

David Alexander Carroll II, Assistant Clerk

Moses Lalane, CFO

Esther Louis Lalane, Treasurer

Jean Bradley Derenoncourt, Delegate

Luc Junior Buissereth, Advisor

Onel Berrette, Second Advisor

Denis Michel, Director

Jessy Rene Louis, Vice Director

Boston, August 12th, 2019

PROJECT IDEA

ERADICATION OF CONFLICT AND VIOLENCE IN BOSTON, MASSACHUSETTS

NOTE: *We are currently finalizing a detailed budget of the project and preparing to contact potential donors. As you consider this project idea, we will be making consultations in-field and conducting further research in order to fully develop the project.*

Wilson Thelimo Louis, President/CEO of ITIAHaiti

BRIEFING

This project involves the launching of an educational and recreational program for young Haitians in Boston, Massachusetts to promote wholesome recreation, self-esteem, and increased educational and professional opportunities. Because many youths in Massachusetts experience violence, this project will teach peaceful conflict resolution skills to enable youth to eradicate violence in their homes and communities. Participants will first learn to identify the different forms of violence (verbal, physical, emotional, etc.) and conflict existing in Massachusetts (political, socioeconomic, familial, workplace, etc.); they will then work in groups with other youth to propose preventative measures to conflict and violence.

OUR FOCUS

When analyzing the political crisis, discrimination, and stigmatization against black communities, and economic instability which have marginalized the majority of Massachusetts' Haitian population, it becomes apparent that these conditions have led to an increase in violence against immigrants, including exploitation, human trafficking, theft, assault, and rape, etc. The target group for this commitment includes young immigrants in the community most at risk of experiencing violence, including women, and children, especially those in economically depressed situations. Some of them are "just come" in the

United States of America and have been incarcerated from their own people and not be able to have access to public services because of lack of knowledge on navigating into the American system.

OUR MISSION

For this commitment, we will offer an educational program to the Haitian youth in Boston, Massachusetts during the summer vacations, which lasts from early June to the end of August. Participants will be recruited during the preceding months through networks such as schools, churches, and community organizations of Massachusetts. Also, government institutions, businesses, and nonprofit organizations will be solicited for material and institutional support during this period. The program will then begin in June with training sessions and group discussions held biweekly at the ITIAHaiti's campus in Boston. Seminars will focus on the eradication of violence and conflict as it exists in Massachusetts. Group discussions will be based on violence, conflict management, social cohesion, and peaceful conflict resolution. Since many youths learn effectively through applied teaching techniques, the program will also include sports and artistic components. The sports program will consist of basketball, soccer, volleyball, and ping pong tournaments, during which we will focus on teaching the concept of fair play and conflict prevention to Haitian immigrants. In the art program, artistically-minded youth can create paintings, musical compositions, theatrical plays, and other works of art to express their views and opinions on violence and conflict resolution. Similarly, we will organize singing, dancing, poetry, and drawing competitions to engage youth in discussions about how to address issues of violence and oppression in their society. At the end of the three-month program, a graduation ceremony will be held to showcase young peoples' achievements, and certificates will be distributed to participants.

HOW THIS PROJECT IS DIFFERENT
FROM OTHER

As community mentors and volunteers, we have collaborated extensively with area schools, churches, and organizations to inform young people about sexually transmitted diseases, HIV/AIDS, reproductive health, self-worth, and drug prevention. Throughout these experiences, it has become apparent to us that many local and international nonprofit organizations, as well as government agencies, are very interested in educational projects on conflict resolution and the eradication of violence. Churches, schools, and nonprofits are eager to implement such programs because they will help build a more cohesive society. This project differs from past programs we have been involved in because we have never before led an educational program on violence awareness. In addition to being a new project, this initiative will also incorporate innovative ideas such as the importance of the individual as part of a collective group in conflict resolution. Thus, the program will focus on both individual expression and group discussion.

OUR SUCCESS

Level of success for this commitment will be determined through several key indicators, including funds raised, number of enrolled participants, attendance at biweekly discussion groups, and participation in sporting and artistic events. The percentage of enrolled participants who complete the program and receive a certificate will also be a good indicator of program success. To conduct a more qualitative evaluation, we will ask participants to complete a closing survey in which they rate the effectiveness of the program and share their comments and suggestions. As part of the survey, we will also ask participants to share any experiences they had over the course of the summer in which they were able to apply the conflict resolution skills they learned in the seminars. These surveys will be evaluated to determine what aspects of the program were popular among the participants and what should be changed for the next year.

EXPECTATIONS

Violence is a problem encountered by far too many people in our society, especially girls, women, and children. Unfortunately, this issue is often overlooked and not discussed openly in national arenas. To resolve this problem, this project should be part of an integrated effort to eradicate violence by mobilizing Bostonians youth and giving them the training they need to become community educators, fieldworkers, and specialists. These youth will then be able to implement further programs which will help increase the public consensus about violence, improve human communication in resolving conflicts, and mobilize government leaders to improve the situation of human rights in the

City. This commitment will enable young people to lead such efforts in our community. The artistic works they produce during the program will be on display for others in the community to learn about young people's ideas on peace and eradication of violence. Also, young people who complete our program will be able to teach their parents the principles they have learned. The project structure will include administration, human resources, equipment, backup plans for unforeseen events, follow-up, evaluation, teaching, and training.

William Francis Galvin
Secretary of the
Commonwealth

The Commonwealth of Massachusetts
Secretary of the Commonwealth
State House, Boston, Massachusetts 02133

Date: August 26, 2019

To Whom It May Concern :

I hereby certify that according to the records of this office,

ITIAHAITI NONPROFIT CORPORATION

is a domestic corporation organized on **August 22, 2019**

I further certify that there are no proceedings presently pending under the Massachusetts General Laws Chapter 180 section 26 A, for revocation of the charter of said corporation; that the State Secretary has not received notice of dissolution of the corporation pursuant to Massachusetts General Laws, Chapter 180, Section 11, 11A, or 11B; that said corporation has filed all annual reports, and paid all fees with respect to such reports, and so far as appears of record said corporation has legal existence and is in good standing with this office.

In testimony of which,
I have hereunto affixed the
Great Seal of the Commonwealth
on the date first above written.

Secretary of the Commonwealth

Certificate Number: 19080485070
Verify this Certificate at: http://corp.sec.state.ma.us/CorpWeb/Certificates/Verify.aspx
Processed by:

TABLE OF CONTENTS

CHAPTER III:

CHAPTER IV:

CHAPTER V: RESPONSIBILITIES

CONTACT US

Phone: +1 786-659-3961

E-mail: itiahaiti@yahoo.fr

You can also purchase Kindles, Paperbacks and

Audiobooks published by ITIAHaiti on:

www.amazon.com/author/thelimo

L'AMOUR ET LA PASSION, collection de Poèmes

L'ECHO DES CAYES, Recueil de nouvelles

www.itiahaiti.org

itiahaiti@itiahaiti.org

CC404096

City of Boston
Office of the City Clerk
Toom, 1001C

RECEIVED
CITY C□□□□ □□ICE

*19 JUL 24 P 3:38

BOST□ □□□□

BUSINESS CERTIFICATE - Filing Fee: $65.00

☑ New Filing ☐ Renewal

This Certificate Expires on: JUL 24 2023

Under the provisions of Chapter 110, Section 5 of the Massachusetts General Laws, as amended, the undersigned hereby declares that a business under the title of:

ITIAHAITI   is being conducted at:
(Please Print Clearly)

45 Stanbro Street   BOSTON   MA   02136
(P.O. Box not permitted)   (City)   (State)   (Zip Code)

By the following individual (s) or Corporation   Corporation or Residential Address
Print Full Name (s)   (P.O. Box not permitted)

Wilson Thelmo Louis   45 Stanbro Street, Hyde Park, MA 02136

Signature:

Individuals MUST have their signatures notarized on the back of this form prior to filing in the Office of the City Clerk.

Local Telephone Number: (786) 659-3961   Type of Business: Litterary Organization

Email Address: itiahaiti@yahoo.fr   Website:

IMPORTANT NOTICE

This Certificate expires four (4) years from the date of issue. If you cease conducting business before that time, the law requires that you withdraw this Certificate with the Office of the City Clerk.

City of Boston Certification

A true copy of the original document filed on the above date in the Office of the City Clerk.

JUL 24 2019   - 3:38 pm

Attest:

City Clerk

The Commonwealth of Massachusetts
Secretary of the Commonwealth
State House, Boston, Massachusetts 02133

William Francis Galvin
Secretary of the
Commonwealth

Date: August 26, 2019

To Whom It May Concern :

I hereby certify that according to the records of this office,

ITIAHAITI NONPROFIT CORPORATION

is a domestic corporation organized on **August 22, 2019**

I further certify that there are no proceedings presently pending under the Massachusetts General Laws Chapter 180 section 26 A, for revocation of the charter of said corporation; that the State Secretary has not received notice of dissolution of the corporation pursuant to Massachusetts General Laws, Chapter 180, Section 11, 11A, or 11B; that said corporation has filed all annual reports, and paid all fees with respect to such reports, and so far as appears of record said corporation has legal existence and is in good standing with this office.

In testimony of which,
I have hereunto affixed the
Great Seal of the Commonwealth
on the date first above written.

William Francis Galvin

Secretary of the Commonwealth

Certificate Number: 19080485070
Verify this Certificate at: http://corp.sec.state.ma.us/CorpWeb/Certificates/Verify.aspx
Processed by:

www.ingramcontent.com/pod-product-compliance
Lightning Source LLC
Chambersburg PA
CBHW030723220526
45463CB00005B/2155

9 781689 152839